AMERICAN ARCADE

"Explosive, exciting...highly charged and hugely fun... bawdy and controversial...taking risks and pushing boundaries. And there are moments of such irreverent joy... that the risks are ultimately justified."
—Alli Marshall, *Mountain Xpress*

"Zany, racy, edgy and over the top... Has Samuels shot himself in the foot with this "Outrage in Two Acts"? A quick answer is "No." This is among his best work. It's a mystery, with Sherlock Holmes' cape, cap and massive magnifying glass. It's a comedy, with Marx Brothers' timing... And it has some moments of high drama...with even some significant psychological if not philosophical elements... This is a study in sanity and insanity... Lots of questions, a few answers and scary moments accented with frequent guffaws."
—Jim Cavener, *Asheville Citizen-Times*

A dark stage comedy about the contemporary American family, business, sexuality, race relations, psychiatry, and organized crime, Steven Samuels' *American Arcade* concerns the Hamlet-like Harry Hunter, a young manufacturer of old-fashioned shooting gallery games struggling to sustain his beloved past, his family, and what remains of his sanity while the confounding present explodes in his face.

Also published by The Sublime Theater & Press

My Crazy My Love
by John Crutchfield

Washington Place
by David Brendan Hopes

AMERICAN ARCADE;
or,
How To Shoot Yourself in the Face
(An Outrage in Two Acts)

STEVEN SAMUELS

THE SUBLIME THEATER & PRESS
Asheville, NC

American Arcade; or, How To Shoot Yourself in the Face
Copyright © 2021 by Steven Samuels

Published by The Sublime Theater & Press, Inc.
49 Faircrest Road, Asheville, NC 28804-1848
ss@thesublimetheater.org

The Sublime Theater & Press, Inc. is a 501(c)(3) tax-exempt organization.

All rights reserved. Except for brief passages quoted in newspaper, magazine, radio, television, or online reviews, no part of this book may be reproduced in any form or by any means, electronic or mechanical, including photocopying or recording, or by an information storage and retrieval system, without permission in writing from the publisher.

Professionals and amateurs are hereby warned that this material, being fully protected under the Copyright Laws of the United States of America and all other countries of the Berne and Universal Copyright Conventions, is subject to a royalty. All rights including, but not limited to, professional, amateur, recording, motion picture, recitation, lecturing, public reading, radio and television broadcasting, online presentation, and the rights of translation into foreign languages, are expressly reserved. Particular emphasis is placed on the question of readings and all uses of this book by educational institutions. Inquiries concerning production rights for this play should be addressed to the publisher.

ISBN 978-1-952720-02-4 (Hardcover)
ISBN 978-1-952720-00-0 (Paperback)
ISBN 978-1-952720-01-7 (E-book)

First edition, May 2021

American Arcade; or, How To Shoot Yourself In the Face (An Outrage in Two Acts), was first presented by The Magnetic Theatre at 375 Depot Street, Asheville, NC, on June 8, 2017.

Written and Directed by Steven Samuels
Assistant Directed by Rodney Smith
Set Design by Kirstin Leigh Daniel
Master Carpentry by Erik Moellering
Costume Design and Choreography by Elizabeth Evans
Lighting Design by Jason Williams
Stage Management by Samara Ross-Halleck

CAST
(in order of appearance)
Harry Hunter…Cody Magouirk
Veronica Wilson…Elizabeth Evans
Ray Hunter…Darren Marshall
Angela Hunter…Sophia Mosby
Theodora Hunter…Tippin
Patricia Hunter…Jane Hallstrom
Dr. Frechette…Terry Darakjy
Anthony Little…Steven Samuels
Franklin Robinson…Dakota Mann

TIME: Today.

SETTING: The office of The American Arcade Company and, briefly, a psychiatrist's office.

CAST (in order of appearance)
HARRY HUNTER, a businessman
VERONICA WILSON, Harry's assistant
RAY HUNTER, Harry's father (deceased)
ANGELA HUNTER, Harry's daughter
THEODORA HUNTER, Harry's wife
PATRICIA HUNTER, Harry's mother
DR. FRECHETTE, Harry's psychiatrist
ANTHONY LITTLE, a mobster
FRANKLIN ROBINSON, Veronica's fiancé
THUGS (all actors but Harry)
ATTENDANT (actor who plays Ray)

NOTES ON THE SET: Stage right: a downstage door to the office of The American Arcade Company, with its simple couch, desk and chair, a corded telephone, and an upstage exit to a hallway leading to restrooms and the coffee room. Dominating the stage: a wall painted with the ducks, bears, tin cans, stars, what-have-you, that might have been seen in an arcade shooting gallery in the 1950s. Carved into the wall, asymmetrically and at various heights: eight head-sized slots that can be opened and shut. Within the wall: a panel or panels that can be raised or retracted to reveal a rolling cart, pushed forward as needed, adorned with a fainting couch and an armchair, for the psychiatrist's office. Above the wall, two signs: "AMERICAN ARCADE CO." and its slogan: "Come on! Take a shot!"

PRONUNCIATION NOTE: The acronym for the American Arcade Company—AAC—is pronounced "ack."

AMERICAN ARCADE

ACT ONE

HARRY HUNTER, dressed in camo, makes his way through the audience, leading with a toy rifle.

Harry:
Don't look at me! Don't call me paranoid!
I'm not telling you the world's against me;
I've got some specifics. War is coming.
We all know that. It always is. But now:
It comes now! It's upon us already.
Like a Boy Scout, be prepared. Grab a gun.
Protect yourself. Protect your family
And your friends, assuming you have any.
Assume nothing. What was will be no more;
What was good, I mean. What was bad comes back;
What I had thought done. I just couldn't see:
Hate never ends, nor the will to power.
Faith in country, people, progress: betrayed.
Likewise trust in loved ones: wife and mother;
Daughter; dead father, gone before his time.
Business associates. Business itself.
No one cares about my deepest concerns,
Though I do theirs. Happiness? Ha! Pleasure?
We won't have that! Or I won't, anyway,
Not of the physical variety.
Nothing remains unless it's digitized,
Except harm: to the planet, your person.
Oh, I was happy and would be again
If our greed and madness came to an end.
The universe doesn't care that I'm here,
So trust me: I have reason to be scared.
They're coming for me. They're gunning for me.
God damn me if I go down easily!

By now, Harry has made his way onto the stage;

or, rather, into the office of The American Arcade Company, where his assistant, VERONICA WILSON, dressed nicely in business casual, eyes him warily.

Veronica: Mr. Hunter?

Harry: Harry, please. Haven't we been working together several months already?

Veronica: Sorry. It's just the way I was raised.

Harry: Let's not stand on ceremony.

Veronica: All right...Harry. May I ask: are you all right?

Harry: Never better. Why?

Veronica: I don't know. You're here early. You seem agitated. You're carrying a rifle.

Harry: What? This? It's a prototype!
(Places rifle on the wall. Removes camo, which he stashes in a desk drawer, revealing himself in business very *casual: a button-down, short-sleeved shirt; slacks—not jeans; loafers; and a tie hung so loosely around his neck the knot bangs against his breastbone)*
A new idea I'm testing. You've got to move forward or you're a big behind!
(Laughs. Veronica tries to laugh, too. Harry joins her by the desk)
And how are you, Veronica? Getting comfortable here at The American Arcade Company, AAC?

Veronica: Am I comfortable...?

Harry: I know how hard it can be adjusting to a new environment. Easier for you than it would have been for...a person of color? A black? An African American? Do you know what those people call themselves these days? I wouldn't want to make a mistake!

Veronica: Those people? Mr. Hunter...

Harry: *(Wagging his finger)* Uh uh uh! We're friends, aren't we, as much as colleagues? God, can you imagine if I'd hired a person of color who called me "boss?" "Yessuh, boss!": there's one we don't need to hear!

Veronica: Oh dear.

Harry: No offense, but I wish you were black! I believe reparations should be paid, and that could have been my way of giving back, of acknowledging and dealing with my white privilege!

Veronica: I'm sorry you didn't get to take...affirmative action? I guess you hired me for my abilities.

Harry: No, you were the only one who applied. But I'm glad it worked out this way, really, Veronica: you're steadfast, reliable, strong...

Veronica: I try to be...

Harry: And you succeed! In just a few short months, you've made yourself indispensable to AAC, the only supplier of old-fashioned shooting gallery games in the U.S. of A.!

Veronica: I'm glad!

Harry: Me too.

Veronica: Because I have to ask... I was wondering...

A slot in the wall opens and RAY HUNTER's head appears in it. One of his temples has sustained a horrifying gunshot wound. To the extent we can see his shirt, it's blood-soaked.

Ray: And so it begins...

Harry: Daddy?

Ray: It's always about money.

Harry: It's not always about money!

Ray: Don't say I didn't warn you. *(Closes slot)*

Veronica: It's about money, Harry. Can I get an advance? To tide me over till my next pay period?

Harry: You tell me. You keep the books.

Veronica: I think if our overdue payments come through...

She starts pawing through papers.

Ray: *(Opens slot)* It's probably good you hired her. What could you have gotten out of a colored woman, except maybe sex?

Harry: Oh my god, Dad! Stop saying racist shit!

Ray: You think all that stuff you hear about them being lazy is just a cliché? Didn't I tell you clichés are clichés for a reason? And by the way, this girl may not be black, or even Asian, but she's pretty hot for a white chick! Have you slept with her yet?

Harry: Dad!

Ray: Trust me, she's ready to go. Is there a problem?

Harry: Let's start with I'm married!

Ray: I was married, too, but I never let that stop me. Never turn down a chance to sleep with a willing woman!

Harry: Well, Dad, there's an odds-on chance we're not the same.

Ray: Okay, but if I were you? I'd try to be a lot more like me. *(Closes slot)*

Harry: Dead of a gunshot to the head at 45? An apparent suicide?

Ray: *(Opens slot)* Hey! You don't know how I died, apart from the shot-in-the-head part. I know you've considered other possibilities: a mob rubout, a freak assembly-line accident... But you could be right about suicide. I had money troubles that would have made the mob kill me if I didn't kill myself! Or I might have been in suicidal despair about the relentless downward spiral of AAC. And, you know, I thought your mom was cheating on me, I won't say with who. And I always felt I failed you as a father. I did not die happy about your future.

Harry: I love my life, Dad. I thank you for it. I'm gonna make everything work out!

Ray laughs, closes slot. Veronica looks up from her papers, fixes Harry with her eyes.

Veronica: Now that I've looked more closely, I don't know how we can press for payment with so many unresolved complaints.

Harry: Unresolved?

Veronica: Slow response times. Machines down for months. Some of our customers are threatening to sue.

Harry: Traveling carnies, Midwest state fairs, the last few true arcades... No judge will take them seriously!

Veronica: They all complain about Repairman Dan. They say he's a drunk.

Harry sinks to the couch.

Harry: Oh, Repairman Dan...

Veronica: I know you're devoted to him, but even I can see... And I know someone who'd do such a good job! He's smart, hardworking, he's got several college degrees, including engineering, and he's great to be around!

Harry: Who is this miracle man?

Veronica: My fiancé, Franklin Robinson.

Harry: I didn't know you were engaged! Congratulations! Better put in for your honeymoon soon. When's the big day?

Veronica: We haven't set a date yet. We're waiting for Frank to get a job.

Harry: Well, I won't fire Repairman Dan, but maybe there's a way... I don't have anything scheduled today, do I?

Veronica: Not really. But please keep your appointment with Dr. Frechette. You're so much better after!

Harry: Not today. I've got to be here for a call that could solve all our problems!
(The door opens. ANGELA HUNTER storms in, aimed straight at the couch, smartphone in hand. She's dressed for high school, a cool geek)
Sweetheart!

Harry reaches to embrace her. She ducks beneath his arms and throws herself into a corner of the couch, texting. THEODORA HUNTER appears at the door. She's very put together, plainly pays close attention to her appearance.

Theodora: *(To Angela)* You could pretend to give a rat's ass about your dad.

Angela: Like that's ever gonna happen.

Harry: Hey, hey, good to see you, my loves! To what do I owe the pleasure of this unexpected visit?

Veronica: Lovely to see you, Mrs. Hunter, Angela.

Angela turns away. Theodora ignores Veronica's greeting.

Harry: Hey, wait! Shouldn't Angela be at school?

Angela: Why would I want to go to school?

Theodora: We were on our way; but, when I stopped to get cash for her school trip, guess what?

Harry: The transaction didn't go through.

Theodora: *(Overlapping)* The transaction didn't go through!

Angela: We were already late. They must have left already. Can't I hang out here today, Dad? It's not like anyone comes in or you and Veronica do anything, so I wouldn't be in the way!

Harry: Maybe if you put your phone away...

Theodora: For god's sake, Harry, computers and screens are not ruining everything, and Angel's phone has nothing to do with the destruction of her brain! She's going to school! Better she miss the trip and actually learn something, so she can improve her grades and maybe get the full-ride scholarship to college she needs because her improvident father will never be able to pay her way!

Angela: Stops you cold right there, doesn't she, Dad?

Ray: *(Opens slot)* College? Paying for your business degree almost killed me! You don't want to know what I had to do to pay those bills. And what did it get us? The company's about to go under, which just proves what I hear: college degrees aren't worth shit anymore!

Harry: How can you hear anything? You're dead!

Ray: I have my ways. *(Closes slot)*

Theodora: Let's cut to the chase, Harry. Do we or don't we have any money? How can I get some cash?

Veronica sits on the couch, not too close to Angela.

Veronica: You're sixteen now, aren't you, Angela? Sixteen's great! But it can also be hard. It was a hard time for me—a defining time, too.

Angela: Well, I'm not you.

Ray's slot opens as Veronica returns to her desk, Angela returns to her phone, and Theodora plops down on the couch and pulls out her own phone.

Ray: Your daughter's lovely, Harry. Delectable. Yum.

Harry: Dad! You can't talk that way about your own granddaughter!

Ray: I'm not supposed to notice her sweet knockers?

Harry: Don't you dare notice her knockers! And don't talk about them—not to me!

Ray: You can't tell me you haven't noticed her sweet knockers! *(Closes slot)*

Angela: Dad, if you just give me the money you would have paid for my class trip, I can go out with my friends instead of always being stuck at home with you and mom!

Ray: *(Opens slot)* Don't give her any money! That's a slippery slope.

Theodora: *(To Harry)* If your father had left you anything besides his failing business; if he had died in any other way than suicide, so we could have collected on his life insurance policy...

Ray: Oh, Theodora! How she loved me!

Angela: *(To Harry)* You talk about your dad like he was an angel.

Harry: You're the Angel! But my dad was a good guy.

Ray: I was.

Harry: We had fun.

Ray: We did!

Angela: Well, I never knew him.

Ray: You were too young when I died. You're pretty much the only reason I'm sorry I'm dead. Pardon my French, son, but your wife's still a bitch.

Harry: Dad, lay off Theo or you'll have to stop haunting me!

Ray: I told you she was frigid.

Harry: She's wonderful! I love her!

Ray: All she's done is saddle you with a kid who disrespects you and give you the longest case of blue balls in human history! *(Closes slot)*

Harry tries to sit on the couch between Theodora and Angela, who squirm away.

Harry: We're cash-strapped right now, T, but AAC is perfectly positioned for better days. People want connection. They're turning away from the virtual to the real. There's a new retro wave AAC will ride! I'm working on a very big deal!

Theodora: *(Placing a hand over his, simulating affection)* Harry, love, are you seeing Dr. Frechette today?

Angela: Who's Dr. Frechette?

Ray: *(Opens slot)* Your daughter doesn't know you see a shrink?

The door opens and PATRICIA HUNTER enters. If anything, her clothes, hair, and makeup are more together than Theodora's, which are a comparatively cheap imitation.

Patricia: Harry, we need to talk!

Ray: Uh-oh. Gotta go! *(Closes slot)*

Harry: *(Leaping up)* Mom!

Patricia: Oh—Theo, Angela! I didn't expect to see you!

Veronica: *(Rising)* Hello, Mrs. Hunter.

Theodora: *(Getting up and pulling Angela up with her)* We were just leaving, Patricia.

Patricia: Not until I get a hug from my darling Angela!

Angela: *(Submitting to Patricia's embrace)* Oh, Grandma, please convince mom to let me skip school today! Can't I be with you? I never get to see you!

Theodora: Let's go, Ange!

Patricia: Theodora, loosen up! Ordinarily, I wouldn't let Angela play hooky, but there's more than one kind of education. Why don't we three girls go to lunch? My treat! After I go the ladies'. Who's with me?

Veronica: I'll come with you, Mrs. Hunter.

Patricia: Veronica, please. I'm not so old that I can't go to the bathroom on my own!

Veronica: No! I've got to go, too!

Patricia: Well, don't let me stop you.

Patricia and Veronica exit into the hallway. Angela plops back down onto the couch.

Angela: God, I hate grandma!

Harry: Angela!

Angela: I hate everything about her: how she dresses, how she talks. I hope to god I'm nothing like her when I'm old!

Harry: She's only in her sixties! That's not old!

Angela: Says you.

A new wall slot opens. Patricia's head appears.

Patricia: Oh, but that Angela's a doll! What a good father you are, Harry!

Ray: *(Opens slot)* Fancy meeting you here, Patty Pie!

Patricia: Don't talk to me, Ray. You're dead!

Ray: You were always dead to me, sexually. You neglected me the way Theo neglects Harry. History repeats but worsens, because Harry isn't smart enough to get himself some!

Patricia: Animal!

Ray: You're the one bleeding the poor boy dry. Your spendthrift ways almost took me under!

Patricia: Was I supposed to sit around waiting for you to come home while you ran wild with your whores?

Harry: Mom! Dad! Stop fighting, please!

Both slots close.

Theodora: Angela, let's go before your grandmother comes back. *(To Harry)* The more I know her, the less surprised I am by how you turned out!

Patricia: *(Opens slot)* Don't put this off on me, missy! I didn't raise Harry to be a loser! I gave him unconditional love! I'm not sure you love him at all! *(Closes slot)*

Theodora drags Angela to the door.

Theodora: Your "big deal" better not be a fantasy, Harry. Don't bother coming home tonight without *beaucoup de* bucks!

Harry: You're leaving without even saying goodbye to my mother?

Theodora pulls Angela out the door. Veronica returns to her desk. Patricia reenters.

Patricia: What happened to the girls?

Harry: Theo insisted on taking Angela to school.

Patricia: *(Settling onto the couch)* Oh, that makes me sad! I was so looking forward to a little time with Angela; Theo, not so much.

A wall slot opens. Theodora's head appears.

Theodora: Oh, Harry. If only I could learn to be more like your amazing mother!

Another wall slot opens. Angela's head appears.

Angela: Totally! I want to be just like her when I grow up. If only she could have been my mother!

Theodora: Angela!

Their slots close.

Patricia: You and Theo spoil Angela rotten! She should know how hard my life was when I was her age, how foolish I was to marry your horrible father...

Harry: Mom...

Patricia: ...and to have had you so young. But I did what I could for you...

Harry: I'm sorry, Mom. When I think about the trouble I gave you when I was sixteen...

Patricia: You're worse now! Your father may have been a rotten louse, but at least he provided! You know why I came here this morning? To make sure you're paying my bills! I was planning to lunch with the ladies today and I did not want to be embarrassed again by having my credit card declined!

Harry: I'm doing everything I can! If you could occasionally restrain yourself, maybe not rush out to buy the latest fashions and dine out morning, noon, and night...

Patricia: You want me to live on dog food and dress like a tart, like your wife?

Veronica: Can I get anyone coffee?

Harry and Patricia: No thanks!

Veronica exits into the hallway. A wall slot opens. DR. FRECHETTE's head appears.

Dr. Frechette: When you come in for your appointment later, Harry, let's talk about your mother. I think she's the source of all your problems.

Harry: Not my father's violent, mysterious death?

Her slot closes.

Patricia: Harry, why does your assistant have to be so attractive?

Harry: Is she? I never noticed.

Patricia: Are you sure you're your father's son?

Harry: Wouldn't you know?

A wall slot opens. Veronica's head appears.

Veronica: I love your mother, Harry. She says the sweetest things! *(Closes slot)*

Patricia: My god, I've got to pee again! The indignities of age...

She heads for the hallway.

Harry: *(Following)* You're joking about me not being daddy's son, right, Mom?

When everyone's gone, the door opens. ANTHONY LITTLE appears, dressed like a black-and-white-movie mobster.

Anthony: Anybody home?

Veronica returns, freezes.

Veronica: May I help you?

Anthony: I bet you could! But is this AAC?

Veronica: AAC, yes...

Anthony: Is Harry Hunter here?
(Harry returns, stops short)
I'd recognize you anywhere, son, though I haven't seen you since Ray had to hold you up to shoot the ducks and bears and stars! What, you don't remember me? Have I changed that much? Don't answer that! Time's been cruel—at least to me. Speakin' of which, how's your mother? How's your father?

Harry: You knew my father?

Ray: *(Opens slot)* Oh, he knew everything about me... *(Closes slot)*

Harry: My father passed away fifteen years ago.

Anthony: I had no idea! Was it sudden?

Harry: As sudden as a gunshot to the head!

Anthony: Oh!

Harry: Some say it was suicide...

Anthony: That ain't the Ray Hunter I know!

Harry: Knew.

Anthony: How's your poor mother?

Harry: She adjusted surprisingly quickly.

Patricia returns, startled to see Anthony. She swiftly approaches with the warmest of smiles.

Patricia: I don't believe it!

She offers Anthony her hands.

Anthony: Patricia, you look wonderful!

Patricia: You're looking pretty sharp yourself, Anthony! What brings you here after all these years?

Ray: *(Opens slot)* I was wondering that myself!

Anthony: I happened to be in the neighborhood, so I thought I'd drop by. I been livin' on the West Coast, but I just moved back!

Patricia: Oh, that's interesting!

Ray: Very!

Anthony: I'm sorry to hear about Ray.

Ray: Really?

Patricia: Oh, that was so long ago...

Ray: See the light of love in their eyes? I always wondered if they were doing it behind my back! *(Closes slot)*

Harry: *(Clears his throat)* So you're Anthony...?

Anthony: Just Anthony. It's safer that way.

FRANKLIN ROBINSON appears at the door, dressed in a pleasant-enough suit and tie, down-at-the-heels job-interview clothes.

Franklin: Oh, sorry. Is this...

Veronica races to him and begins hustling him back out the door.

Veronica: Frankie, I didn't tell you to just drop in!

Franklin: I thought you wanted me...

Harry: Frankie? This is Franklin Robinson? He's your fiancé?

Veronica: You sound surprised. Isn't he cute? He's adorable!

Harry: No, it's just—well, his name, I thought...

Veronica: I'm sorry, Harry. I didn't expect him to just barge in like this!

Harry: And I didn't expect him...
(Shakes Franklin's hand, draws him into the room)
So you're Veronica's fiancé! I'm Harry, Harry Hunter, head of AAC. This is my mother, Patricia...

Franklin: Pleased to meet you.

Harry: ...and our old family friend, Anthony...?

Anthony: Just Anthony.

Franklin: How do you do?

Anthony: Very well, I thank you. Ding dong ding!

Anthony and Patricia laugh familiarly.

Patricia: Oh, Anthony! Such a card!

Anthony: Ah, what the hell? They're civilians. The name's Anthony Little, and, yeah, they call me "Little Anthony," which is fine by me as long as nobody makes smart remarks!

Patricia: Remember Little Anthony and the Imperials? "Tears on My Pillow"? "Goin' Out of My Head"?

Anthony: "Shimmy, Shimmy, Ko-Ko-Bop"?

Franklin: "Hurt So Bad"! *(Sings)* "Well let me tell you that it..."
(Patricia and Anthony become the Imperials to Fanklin's Little Anthony as they sing and dance to the end of the song's chorus)
Of course I remember Little Anthony and the Imperials! I'm a big R&B fan!

Veronica: Me too!

Ray: *(Opens slot)* See, Harry? Everyone's got a taste for chocolate! *(Closes slot)*

Patricia: Anthony used to manage them!

Franklin: Really?

Patricia: Where do you think they got their name?

Anthony: Pat, I never managed them, not on paper! Let's just say they worked for me.

Veronica: And speaking of working...

Franklin: Very, this isn't the time...

Veronica: Seize the day, Frankie! Harry: face facts! AAC is faltering because Dan's too soused to get the job done!

Patricia: Oh, Repairman Dan...

Anthony: I remember Repairman Dan! He could really put it away!

Ray's slot opens.

Harry and Ray: I love him!

Ray's slot closes.

Harry: He's the one who got me through when Dad passed away!

Patricia: I know, honey, but you can't keep living in the past!

Veronica: And you've got an opportunity with Franklin to get AAC back on track!

Anthony: Listen, son. I know all about loyalty. But when it comes to business, you can't let anyone or anything stand in your way!

Harry: I can't just fire Repairman Dan!

Veronica: I bet you'd hire Frank if he were black!

Harry: What? No! But okay: if what I'm hoping happens happens today, AAC's gonna grow and we'll have to staff up. It all depends on that call I'm expecting...

The telephone rings. Everyone looks at it.

Veronica: *(Answering)* American Arcade Company, Veronica speaking... Let me see if he's available. May I put you on hold, Mr. Brewster? Thank you... Harry, it's a Mr. Brewster from Out-of-the-Past Productions...

Harry: This is it this is it this is it...

Patricia: This is what?

Franklin: This is what?

Anthony: This is what?

Harry: You've heard of Dave & Buster's? Chuck E. Cheese's? These guys wanna be that with the classic arcade games AAC specializes in! They've got the capital to launch a hundred locations over the next three years. If we become a supplier, AAC will be bigger than ever!

Patricia: How wonderful that would be!

Anthony: I'm surprised I never heard of this Out-of-the-Past...

Veronica: Harry? Are you gonna take the call?

Franklin: Good luck!

Veronica: Harry?

Patricia: Harry?

Harry: I can't! I just can't! Tell him I'm unavailable! Ask him to call back!

Patricia: Harry!

Anthony: What's wrong with you, son?

Harry: Veronica, please!

Harry throws himself onto the couch.

Veronica: *(Into the phone)* Sorry to keep you waiting, Mr. Brewster. I'm afraid Mr. Hunter's tied up at the moment. Could you possibly call back this afternoon? *(Looking at Harry)* Two o'clock?
(Harry nods)
Yes, two o'clock should work nicely. Thank you so much, Mr. Brewster. Goodbye. *(Hangs up)* What was that, Harry?

Patricia: Yes, what was that?

Anthony: Jeez, you're lucky he agreed!

Harry: I couldn't breathe! I was paralyzed by hope and...the opposite of hope!

Franklin: Hopelessness. Despair.

Harry: Despair that it might not happen, which could mean the end of AAC!

Patricia: What makes you think you'll be able to take the call when he calls back?

Harry: Because...

Theodora: *(Opens slot)* Your mother doesn't know?

Harry: Why would I tell my mother?

Theodora: You're gonna have to tell her now! *(Closes slot)*

Harry: Mom, if you must know, I'm seeing a psychiatrist. I've got an appointment this morning I hope will help.

Patricia: Oh.

Ray: *(Opens slot)* I don't think she likes this... *(Closes slot)*

Patricia: I suppose he blames everything on me...

Harry: She, Mom, and no. It's nothing like that.

Patricia: Then what is it like?

Anthony: I sure could use some coffee! Anyone else could use some coffee?

Harry: We've got a coffee machine in the back.

Veronica: I forgot to tell you, Harry, it's on the fritz.

Franklin: I could take a look at it...

Anthony: Don't bother! I seen a coffee shop on the corner. What can I get everyone? On me!

Franklin: I can help!

Patricia: Why don't we all go? Take a little break?

Veronica: Sounds fun! Would that be all right, Harry?

Harry: Sure. You go. I'll stay.

Patricia: Alone?

Anthony: You okay?

Harry: What? You think I'm gonna shoot myself, like dad?

> *Harry laughs uncomfortably. The others do, too. Theodora opens the door.*

Theodora: What's so funny?

Patricia: Nothing, just a little... Theodora, this is Anthony Little, an old family friend. Anthony, this is Harry's wife.

Anthony: Ain't he the lucky guy!

Veronica: And this is my fiancé, Franklin.

Franklin: Nice to meet you.

Anthony: Say, we were just goin' out for coffee! Care to join us?

Theodora: Oh. I was hoping to have a word with Harry.

Anthony: Can we bring you anything?

Theodora: I'm fine.

Anthony: OK. Come on everybody!

Anthony opens the door for Patricia and Veronica, then Franklin holds the door for him.

Franklin: After you!

Anthony: Thanks, Frankie!

They exit, leaving Harry and Theodora alone.

Harry: Angel get to school all right?

Theodora: Except that she's not speaking to me. *(Taking the couch)* I loathe your mother, Harry! She spends so much money! She has no regard for you or me or how we're raising Angela! How can you still love her? Even giving birth to you can't make up for her being so selfish and mean!

Harry: You don't mean that, T!

Theodora: And Veronica! Can't I do her job? We could use that salary. And I don't like the way she looks at you. She's a sexy little thing, isn't she?

Harry: For god's sake, Theodora, I'm devoted to you! And you just met her fiancé! She hopes he'll work here, too!

Theodora: Just what we need: another mouth to feed. And who is this Anthony Little?

Harry: He knew my father!

Theodora: He looks like a gangster.

Harry: T! Why would my mother associate with a gangster? Why would dad?

Theodora: Harry, do you even know what business you're in?

Harry: OK, I've gotta go. Unless you want me to be late for my appointment.

Theodora: I bet Dr. Frechette blames everything on me. I bet all you two talk about is sex!

Harry: Given our sex life, there's nothing to discuss.

Theo storms out the door, almost knocking over Anthony, returning.

Anthony: Whoa whoa whoa! What's with her?

Harry: Just a little argument. You know how it is.

Anthony: No, not really, but you'll want to straighten that out right quick. She's really somethin', huh? And don't take that the wrong way, please! I got nothin' but the highest regard for Theodora, and you should, too, because she's a wife and mother! Anyway, I just come back to see if you're sure I can't get you anything.

Harry: I'm sure. Thanks.

Anthony: Also so we can talk.

Harry: About what?

Anthony: Look, I understand things ain't exactly going well for AAC.

Harry: In a world gone digital, I'm trying to keep it real!

Anthony: Well, maybe I can help. For the sake of your mother and in your dear father's memory, I'd like to make things easier for you. I used to make things easier for your dad, too.

Harry: How?

Anthony: Let's just say I used to toss a little business his way.

Harry: No offense, but that sounds shady...

Anthony: Look, kid, I got nothin' to hide!

Harry: You're not in the mob, are you?

Anthony: You kiddin'? A nice Jewboy like me?

Harry: I don't know a lot of Jews named Anthony.

Anthony: Tell the truth, my father was a mobster. He was with the Kosher Nostra. Thought if he named me Anthony...

Harry: Look, Anthony, I don't want to have anything to do with organized crime!

Anthony: Of course not! You think I'd get Pat's son mixed up in a thing like that? No, I'm just a middle man. I could be your silent partner!

Harry: I don't understand.

Anthony: Look. You manufacture toy rifles, don'tcha?

Harry: They're not toys! They're exacting replicas!

Anthony: Whatever. I got friends could use your surplus manufacturin' time, of which I take it you got quite a lot. With just a slight modification, your rifles could suit their needs, you get me?

Harry: Oh no! You're not gonna beat my ploughshares into swords... I mean rifles, functioning rifles! We don't need more violence! Better we play at things than do them!

Anthony: Come on, don't be a useless punk! Violent things are gonna happen with or without you. Why not make a little money for your wife and child and Pat?

Patricia opens the door.

Patricia: Anthony? Is everything all right? You said you'd only be a minute!

Anthony: Sure, sure. Everything's fine. We were just having a nice little chat.

Harry: Sorry. I've gotta run!

Harry leaves the office.

Anthony: That was sudden!

Patricia: He's got an important appointment. With his shrink.

Anthony: No foolin'? A nice young man like that. Well, come on. I suppose we should be gettin' back to Veronica and Frankie.

Patricia: Oh, I felt so out of place with them. They're so young!

Anthony: Tell you what. Why don't the two of us go to lunch—my treat! Catch up on old times.

Patricia: Oh, I don't know. I'm supposed to be lunching with the ladies...

Anthony: Ah, let the ladies hang! The days grow short, Patricia. Fewer and fewer of us are left to remember!

Patricia: I'd like that, Anthony.

As Anthony opens the door for them and they exit, the wall opens and a cart rolls out, with Harry on a couch and Dr. Frechette in an armchair.

Harry: *(Wailing)* No! It's never been worse! Don't you agree?

Dr. Frechette: You tell me.

Harry: So many wars that never end, and how many more on the horizon? A madman in the White House who's dragging us at least 50 years into the past to restore a so-called golden age that was only good for white men, and which will only be good now for rich white men and not even them, because we'll all be choked or sickened or scorched by an environment that just can't take any more, and who cares? My family doesn't care. They won't even talk about it!

Dr. Frechette: Well, it's true most people are caught up in their own *mishegas*...

Harry: *Mishegas?* It's money! That's all they want!

Dr. Frechette: Money...and sex.

Harry: Sex, yes, I guess. Not that I want to think about that, especially when it comes to my daughter...

Dr. Frechette: I appreciate the state of the world upsets you, Harry, but shouldn't you focus on your personal problems? You seem more anxious than ever, and I'd guess you're experiencing a form of transference, substituting worries about the outside world for what's really troubling you underneath.

Harry: What's troubling me underneath is all on the surface!

Dr. Frechette: Like your business woes? You do understand your old-fashioned ways have no future?

Harry: We just keep stepping backward where we need to advance, and moving forward where we need to retrace our steps and start again! Life is not CGI or virtual reality! People need to know this is real!

Dr. Frechette: Like your father's suicide is real? You've still never dealt with that.

Harry: We don't know it was suicide! There was no suicide note!

Dr. Frechette: Suicides don't always leave one. Did he have any enemies?

Harry: How can you help me by driving me crazy?

Ray: *(Opens slot)* What do you expect from a psychiatric professional? Keeping you crazy is how they pay the bills! But believe me, son, you're not nuts. Oh, I know you feel bad. So suck it up! Or, better still, get loaded. Get laid! *(Closes slot)*

Dr. Frechette: Are you still hearing voices?

Harry: What? No!

Dr. Frechette: You're no longer talking to your dead father?

Harry: In my head! Doesn't everyone have little internal conversations with the people in their lives?

Dr. Frechette: But what you've told me about the exchanges with your father sound more like paranoid schizophrenia...

Harry: But I also talk to Theo, Angel, my mother...

Dr. Frechette: Yes, let's talk about your mother...

Patricia: *(Opens slot)* Why is it always the mother? If you'd known his father, you'd realize it's all his fault, even without the suicide! *(Closes slot)*

Dr. Frechette: And understand, I'm not one of those doctors who thinks it's all the mother's fault.

Patricia: *(Opens slot)* Thank you!

Ray: *(Opens slot)* Stop pinning the blame on me!

Patricia: Why not, you miserable lowlife!

Ray: God, this is just like the old days! Me making you unhappy, you saying awful things about me...

Patricia: This is all in Harry's head, but it seems so real!

Ray: I never thought anything happening in Harry's head had the slightest relationship to reality!

Both slots close.

Harry: There's nothing new to say about my mother; you already know how she always belittles me. But, hey, here's a development: an old friend of hers appeared out of the blue today. Anthony Little, or Little Anthony...

Dr. Frechette: What kind of friend?

Harry: Don't start! She couldn't be attracted to him! No man could measure up to my father!

Two slots open: Patricia's and Anthony's.

Anthony: Jeez, he's got an inflated notion of his dad! And, hey, toots, you know I always had the hots for you!

Patricia: Oh, Anthony! How could I have known?

Anthony: How could you not?

Ray: *(Opens slot)* I knew!

All three slots close.

Harry: It's unbelievable! The guy wants to modify my rifles so they can shoot, and sell them to the mob!

Dr. Frechette: You sure you're not making this up?

Harry: He told me himself! Said his father was in the Kosher Nostra!

Dr. Frechette: Now there's a guy I'd like to get on my couch!

Anthony: *(Opens slot)* Oh no! I know how that goes! I seen *The Sopranos*!

Harry: *Analyze This* was funnier.

Anthony: Hey! No funny business!

Ray: *(Opens slot)* No funny business is right, especially not with Patricia!

Anthony: Hey, Ray, nice to see you again!

Ray: What are you doing in my son's head?

Anthony: I thought maybe I could straighten him out!

Ray: Good luck with that.

Both slots close.

Dr. Frechette: Speaking of your mother, how are things going with Veronica?

Harry: What does Veronica have to do with my mother?

Dr. Frechette: Doesn't she try to take care of you, like a mother?

Veronica: *(Opens slot)* I'd love to take care of you, Harry!

Harry: No! You take care of Franklin!

Dr. Frechette: Are you attracted to her? Maybe she's not your office mother. Maybe she's your office wife...

Harry: No!

Ray: *(Opens slot)* She should be!

Veronica: Thanks!

Ray: My pleasure. *(Closes slot)*

Veronica: But, I'm sorry, Harry. Frankie's more than enough lover for me!

Harry: I don't need to know that!

A wall slot opens. Franklin appears.

Franklin: *(Sounding entirely white)* Isn't that just what you need to know, my homie?

Harry: Homie? That's funny. I thought you were black before we met, because of your name, but...

Franklin: I am black. Black is beautiful, man!

Harry: But you're not black. You're white!

Franklin: I am incredibly light-skinned.

Harry: And you don't sound black!

Franklin: You white people. You think all blacks sound alike!

Veronica: That's right!

Veronica's and Franklin's slots close.

Dr. Frechette: How are things with Theodora?

Harry: Oh, you know. The usual.

Theodora: *(Opens slot)* You know I love you, don't you, Harry?

Dr. Frechette: Any progress in the sex department?

Theodora: And how much I want you?

Dr. Frechette: Have you followed through on my suggestion that you encourage her sexuality by discussing and indulging her fantasies?

Theodora: Oh, yes, Harry! Yes! Yes! Yes! *(Closes slot)*

Harry: It's so hard with Angela around.

Dr. Frechette: Is it?

Harry: It's a small apartment. The sound. She'd hear everything!

Dr. Frechette: You don't think she'd be jealous, do you?

Harry: What are you talking about?

Angela: *(Opens slot)* Just divorce mom already, Dad!

Dr. Frechette: Is she a bit of a daddy's girl?

Angela: You're the one who loves me. She just comes between us!

Dr. Frechette: You do know it's natural for a father to engage a—how shall I say?—certain erotic interest in his daughter?

Harry: Only if you're the president...

Angela: I know you're doing all you can for me, Dad! Unlike mom, I don't blame you for us not having money! I believe in your arcade dreams! *(Closes slot)*

Harry: I have absolutely no interest in Angela sexually! And she's a really good kid! She's not into boys or sex or anything, yet!

Anthony: *(Opens slot)* Hey, where is that kid of yours, anyway?

Angela: *(Opens slot)* Hello, Anthony!

Anthony: Whoa! You're a lot more grown up than I expected!

Angela: And you're a big, strong man! You'll help my father, won't you? Ever since his dad died, he's needed a male role model.

Anthony: Let me see what I can do, sweetheart! *(Closes slot)*

Franklin: *(Opens slot)* I'd like to help, too!

Angela: Oh, that would be great! We don't have any people of color in our lives, but I do know black lives matter!

Veronica: *(Opens slot)* Hey: you stay away from my man!

Angela: Veronica! I want to be friends with you, too!

Theodora: *(Opens slot)* You two, stay away from my daughter! *(Veronica's and Franklin's slots close; to Angela)* I don't want you getting any ideas!

Angela: Mom! *(Closes slot)*

Patricia: *(Opens slot)* Hello, Theodora.

Theodora: Patricia. Can't you do something about your son?

Patricia: Can't you do something about your husband?

Angela opens slot, screams. All three slots close.

Dr. Frechette: You know I'm a Freudian analyst. For me, it all comes down to sex.

Harry: I don't want to talk about sex!

Dr. Frechette: When was the last time you and Theodora had relations?

Harry: I don't know. A long time ago.

Dr. Frechette: And that doesn't bother you?

Harry: It bothers me!

Dr. Frechette: I'm wondering about...latency, impulses you may be suppressing. Is it possible you're gay?

Harry: What? No!

Dr. Frechette: Or that you secretly lust after your mother?

Harry: Are you crazy?

Dr. Frechette: Are you asexual? You must want somebody!

Harry: I'll show you who's asexual!

Harry throws himself at Dr. Frechette, forces kisses upon her. She seems to respond, rising and writhing with him. They kiss their way to the couch. Harry climbs on top and, just as they seem to be getting somewhere, she pushes him onto the floor, stands up, straightens her clothes.

Dr. Frechette: Well, that's all we have time for today.

Harry screams, racing into AAC's office as the cart rolls back and the wall is restored.

Harry:
In the end, you're on your own, abandoned
By everyone and crushed by what you wish.
Your parents turn against you or they die.
Love cannot be found or it perishes.
Children, if you have them, go their own way.
Friends learn to hate you, find some other friends.
And god, if you have one, answers no prayers.
Your body can't sustain you, falls apart.
Your sense of self shatters. Your mind decays.

Your dreams go unfulfilled or prove useless.
Nothing remains but the unfounded hope
That strenuous effort will be redeemed.
Once you face facts, why wouldn't you end it?
Abandon all hope, ye who enter here!
And yet, we can't give up, we must go on
As if all of life's lessons will prove wrong.
That there was a purpose, reason to live—
I have to believe that! Wait! Who goes there?
> *(THUGS appear, as if from all directions, hooded, dressed in black, closing in on him, each carrying a weapon or an object that could serve as one: a gun; a knife; a shovel; an ax; the toy rifle grabbed from the wall; a baseball bat; a hockey stick; a lamp)*

What are you doing? What do you want? No, stop! Please! No!
> *(He disappears within their closing circle, screams)*

Mommy!

Blackout.

Act Two

The empty office looks as if the end of Act One never happened. Even the toy rifle is back on the wall.
Harry returns, decked out as the Basil Rathbone Sherlock Holmes, noticeably stewed.

Harry:
The longer I think, the clearer it is
That my father didn't take his own life.
He loved me too much. He loved my mother.
He loved the fun he could provide others,
A fantasy land of entertainment,
The ability to escape their lives,
If only momentarily. Never
For him the sad face or the furrowed brow.
Only ever pleasure, the best of times;
Not for himself alone, but for us all.
Could such a joyous spirit kill himself,
Point a gun at his head, fill it with lead?
I'll never believe it, must clear his name.
The question is: who would have done him in?
He was friends with everyone. They loved him!
This is the mystery his son must solve,
Not only for his reputation's sake;
But because, if his enemy's at large,
He or she may be coming after me,
Might seek my life to remain in the dark.
I must become the greatest detective
The world has ever known, investigate
The crime of my life before it happens,
Identify my father's murderer
Before I become another victim.
But first I think I have to take a nap.
I was so upset after my session

With Dr. Frechette, I'm afraid I drank
Too much at lunch and must pay for it now.

He passes out on the office couch. A slot in the wall opens, revealing Dr. Frechette.

Dr. Frechette: You may be wondering why I've called us all together this afternoon. It's simple, really. Harry's in trouble. He needs our help.

Patricia: *(Opens slot)* What can we do for my poor boy?

Dr. Frechette: You tell me.

Ray: *(Opens slot)* I think his problem is sex.

The remaining slots open.

All but Ray, Dr. Frechette, and Harry: Is it?

Dr. Frechette: Always. For everyone. But especially him.

Anthony: Jeez. When was the last time he was gettin' any on the regular?

All eyes turn to Theodora.

Theodora: Don't look at me!
(All eyes remain on Theodora)
I said don't look at me! I've done my time. He's never satisfied! He's a sex maniac!
(All nod and speak simultaneously: Ray, "That's my son!"; Patricia, "Well, look at his father!"; Angela, "TMI!"; Dr. Frechette, "Hm"; Veronica, "So that's what it is!"; Frank-

lin, "I've noticed that, too!"; Anthony, "That doesn't surprise me!")
Lately, I've been wondering if he's secretly gay. Or transgendered!

All nod again and speak simultaneously: Ray, "Not my son!"; Patricia, "Harry?"; Angela, "Maybe he's just weird"; Dr. Frechette, "Ah!"; Veronica, "It has occurred to me"; Franklin, "Could be"; Anthony, "Huh, I never thought of that!"

Franklin: Well, if that's his problem, maybe I can help. You know, on the DL?

Veronica eyes Franklin, aghast.

Dr. Frechette: Oh, I don't think it's that. Remember, he threw himself at me!

Ray: Probably just trying to prove a point.

Dr. Frechette: Still, if someone would agree to have sex with him...
(All demur and speak simultaneously: Ray, "Not my son!"; Patricia, "Oh, that wouldn't be right"; Theodora, "Someone else, please!"; Angela, "As if!"; Veronica, "Not without a raise!"; Franklin, shaking his head no, "Hm"; Anthony, "Oh no! Don't look at me!" Then all but Dr. Frechette's slots close)
Anyone?

Angela: *(Opens slot)* Well, if you think it would help daddy...

Theodora: *(Opens slot)* Angela, no! That's sick!

Angela: I'd do anything for daddy!

Theodora: For god's sake, can't he even control his fantasies?

The remaining slots open.

All but Theodora and Harry: No!

All slots but Dr. Frechette's close.

Dr. Frechette: That's really disgusting, Angela.

Angela: *(Opens slot)* But you're the one who told him it was normal! You egged him on!

Dr. Frechette: I can't help his thoughts. I was just trying to make him feel better!

Angela: Maybe I can do a better job than you! What's all this "shrinking" done for him, anyway? You've shrunk his self-esteem! You've probably shrunk his junk, too!

The remaining slots open.

All but Angela and Harry: Angela!

Angela: Daddy's the only man I'll ever want!

All but Angela and Harry speak or react simultaneously: Ray, "You have no idea"; Patricia, "Oh, for heaven's sake!"; Theodora, "You could do better"; Dr. Frechette, "Fascinating!"; Veronica fights back upchuck; Franklin makes sounds of revulsion; Anthony, "Oh, that's disgusting!"

Franklin: What about me?

Anthony: And me?

Ray: And me?

Dr. Frechette: Forget it, Ray! Incest is one thing, necrophilia's another, and it's bad to mix the two!

All but Ray and Harry make sounds of revulsion.

Anthony: I can't believe you just said that!

All slots but Dr. Frechette's close.

Theodora: *(Opens slot)* All right. I'll do it. I suppose it's my responsibility.

Patricia: *(Opens slot)* No, Theo, sacrifice is a mother's job. You leave my boy to me!

Ray's and Anthony's slots open.

Ray and Anthony: Pat!

Patricia: It's the least I can do for my son! Besides, it might be fun!

The remaining slots open.

All but Patricia and Harry: Pat!

Veronica: That's all right, Mrs. Hunter. I'll have sex with Harry, if Franklin doesn't mind.

Franklin: It's OK with me, as long as I can watch!

Dr. Frechette: Well, Veronica, Harry does seem to want you.

Veronica: I may not be able to be the black woman he wanted to hire...

Ray: Or an Asian woman...

Veronica: ...or an Asian woman, but we can still play master and slave!

Theodora: Ooh! What about a three-way?

All but Theodora and Harry: Ooh!

All slots but Dr. Frechette's and Veronica's close.

Dr. Frechette: I'm concerned, Veronica, about you turning yourself into other people's fantasies. I may have been projecting about you and Harry. It just may be that I'm the one who wants you!

Veronica: *(Blushing)* Aw, shucks, Dr. Frechette!

Franklin: *(Opens slot)* And if anyone's going to be your lord and master, it should be me!

Veronica: Whatever you say, Frankie!

Franklin: Of course, all white women want me, but since you'll do anything to keep me...

Anthony: *(Opens slot)* Say, I'm beginnin' to see some potential, financially, since all of us are into Veronica. You wouldn't consider pimpin' her out, would you, Frankie? You two could join my stable!

Franklin: Well, I wouldn't mind finding ways to make more than minimum wage. How else can I get in bed with you, Little Anthony?

Anthony: Let's see. You could open up my new gun business to gangstas and thugs, bringin' new meanin' to the term "black market!"

Veronica: I hope this means that we'll get to spend a little time together, Anthony...

Anthony: You bet! And believe me, you'll earn more money workin' the street for me than you ever could as a secretary!

Veronica: Executive assistant.

Anthony: Whatever. All you girls could: Theo...
(Theo's slot opens)
Angela...

Angela's slot opens.

Dr. Frechette: What about me?

Anthony: Of course! The more the merrier!

Patricia: *(Opens slot)* What about me, Anthony?

Anthony: I don't know about that, Pat. What do you think, Frankie? Now that we're partners and all.

Ray: *(Opens slot)* It's your world now, Franklin. We white men surrender. Take our women. Take our money. We deserve whatever you decide to do to us!

The others nod contemplatively.

Angela: I lied when I said I only wanted father, Frankie. You've probably got a bigger one, anyway!

All but Angela, Franklin, and Harry: What? No!

Dr. Frechette: Angela, that's a myth and it's terribly racist!

Franklin: In general, yes, but in this instance...

Ray: Angela, I'm proud of you, even in my grave! Frankie-boy can show you the ropes and Little Anthony's not a bad protector, given his connections!

Angela: And I thought the only organized crime was in the White House! *(Closes slot)*

Theodora: I suppose it's my parental duty to step in and intervene. I can't let Anthony kidnap and sexually enslave my daughter! If only my husband were a man...

Anthony: Dream on, sweetheart. You better submit or you'll end up with nothin'!

Theodora: I guess I wouldn't mind if you'd do the right thing and marry Angela.

Patricia: I don't know how I feel about that!

Theodora: I admit she is a little young, but in some states...

Anthony: I think I begin to understand you, Theodora. I mean, with a husband like Harry... I bet he was awful in the sack—a premature ejaculator, am I right? No wonder you had to turn to vibrators for a little satisfaction. But boy oh boy, if you'd ever let me get my hands on you...

Patricia: Anthony!

Franklin: I bet we could have fun together, too, T!

Veronica: Frankie! No, wait, I'd like to get in on this action, too!

Dr. Frechette: As would I!

Veronica: Ooh! *(Closes her slot)*

Dr. Frechette: You know, I think Harry would like this new you, Theodora. He'd be very excited about your revived sexuality!

Theodora: Except that it's focused on other men—and women!

Patricia: I think I misjudged you, Theodora. I thought you weren't good enough for my Harry, but I realize now you're too good for him!

Ray: And I have a new-found respect for you, too, Theo! I should have known you were right about my son. But I get it now. Go and be happy! You deserve it!

Theodora closes her slot.

Anthony: And I have a new-found respect for you, Dr. Frechette! Baby, there's lots I could teach you you can't learn from books!

Dr. Frechette: Unless they're books on abnormal psychology and sexual deviancy!

Anthony: That a girl!

Dr. Frechette closes her slot.

Patricia: I'm really beginning to feel left out over here! I'm feeling a little age discrimination!

Franklin: Oh, I could "get down" with you, Pat! Lots of men could use a little "mommy time"!

Patricia: Why, thank you, Franklin! Are you going to tie me up and do nasty things to me? I'd like that!

Franklin: We'll see. *(Closes his slot)*

Anthony: Whoa whoa whoa! I don't know how I feel about that, Pat!

Patricia: Oh, Anthony! We're both adults with long, complex histories. Let's have our fun without restricting each other's carnal delights!

Anthony: Believe me, baby, I'll make you feel like no other man can! Have you ever seen god?

Patricia: Can't say that I have.

Anthony: I can make that happen! *(Closes slot)*

Ray: Wait, Anthony! What are you saying to my wife? You think the dead don't have feelings?

Patricia: You're one to complain, Ray! I mean, you're dead! I have the perfect right to sleep with whomever I want! And when I think about how much you cheated...

Ray: Because you'd never have sex with me!

Patricia: We had sex, plenty of sex! If we didn't have sex, how could we have had Harry?

Ray: He only proves we had sex once!

Patricia: You never gave me a tumble after he was born. And fifteen years after your suicide, you think I don't have physical needs?

Ray: I never said I was a suicide!
(Patricia's slot closes)
Though when I think of all the terrible things I did behind your back, and everyone's... You simply would not believe the level of corruption! And my cheating on you, dear Patricia, was simply monumental! And Harry. Poor Harry. How I unmanned him. No wonder he needs Dr. Frechette! Though I wish she'd do something already, prescribe some drugs or lock him away. Enough with the talking! Did I ever tell you, son, about the time Theodora stripped naked and slipped into the shower with me? Come to think of it, that was just before we found out she was pregnant... *(Closes slot)*

Harry: *(Waking up with a shout, falling off of the couch)* What? No! That never happened! None of this happened! You're all insane!

(Veronica stumbles in with Franklin's help; both drunk, she more than he. She falls onto the couch, giggling)
Veronica! You're late! That was a very long lunch!

Veronica: Hey, Harry! Who're you supposed to be?

Harry: Sherlock Holmes. The Basil Rathbone edition.

Veronica: Never heard of him. Are you drunk?

Harry: Not anymore. But you are!

Veronica: We were just celebrating AAC going out of business!

Franklin: Better get some coffee into her.

Harry: There's a coffee machine in the back.

Veronica: It's on the fritz! Everything's on the fritz! What're you investigating, Sherlock?

Harry: My father's death. Whoever's undermining me: is it my mother, my wife, my daughter? Is it you, Veronica?

Veronica: Nope. I'm on your side, Harry, even if I'm beginning to think you have no idea what you're doing. If you did, you'd hire Frankie!

Harry: I'm doing everything I can! Why does everyone always think the problem is me? I'm a nice, thoughtful guy, with the best of intentions and better-than-average follow-through!

Veronica: Says you!

Franklin: Veronica!

Veronica: I'm trying to help you, Frankie!

Franklin: Harry's the one who needs help!

Harry: I'm sorry, Franklin. I just don't think hiring you now is wise!

Franklin: What's wise is letting Repairman Dan destroy what's left of your business?

Harry: Don't you dare say anything against Repairman Dan! That's no way to win friends and influence people!

Franklin: I'm coming to the conclusion that you have no business running AAC!

Harry: Franklin! Who's walking you down this very dark path?

Theodora, also drunk, lurches in, stumbles toward the couch. Angela, stoned, stands in the doorway, sporting a nose ring.

Theodora: *(To Veronica)* Out of my way! Go sit in your chair! There has to be some advantage to being the boss's wife!

Franklin helps Veronica off of the couch. As Theodora collapses onto it, Veronica crawls onto the desk and stretches out.

Harry: Theodora, have you been drinking?

Theodora: I must have been. Why else would I be talking to Sherlock Holmes?

Angela giggles.

Harry: Angela! Are you stoned? What's that in your nose?

Angela: I had to do something during lunch period!

Harry: Theo, did you even notice? What are we going to do about Angela?

Theodora: What are we going to do about anything? It's all over!

Angela: True.

Harry: What's happened to my little Angel? Next thing you know, you'll be getting a tattoo!

Angela: Already have. You want to see it?

She starts to unzip her pants. Harry stops her.

Harry: I can't believe this! My father would never have put up with behavior like this from me!

Angela: I am so sick of hearing about your father! He couldn't have been so great or he wouldn't have left you in this mess!

Theodora: Ray Ray Ray! What a disgusting human being! And a letch. You know he came onto me repeatedly, even when I was pregnant?

Angela: *(To Harry)* And that's the man you worship?

Veronica rolls off of the desk onto her feet, approaches Angela.

Veronica: How dare you speak to your father like that, young lady? If your parents won't discipline you, I will!

Veronica rears back to slap Angela. Franklin stops her.

Angela: Oh, come on, Veronica! Why are you defending dad?

Theodora: He's not even smart enough to hire Frankie!

Harry: Is everyone against me?

Franklin: I'm not against you.

Veronica: I need to lie down!

Franklin helps Veronica back onto the desk. Angela sits in Veronica's chair, fidgets with a pen, papers, the telephone cord. Theodora sits up.

Theodora: So what're we going to do?

Harry: Hope for good news from Out-of-the-Past!

Theodora: And when that doesn't come through?

Harry: I don't know. I suppose I'll have to take Anthony's offer.

Theodora: You want AAC to arm the mob? Give them the guns to kill anyone: you, me, Angela?

Angela: Don't worry about me...

Harry: You're the one telling me I've got to make money, but you undermine everything I try! Still, I love you. I can't help it. No matter what anyone says about you! Sure, we could have more sex...

Angela: Dad, I can hear you!

Harry: Hell, we could have any sex!

Franklin: *(To Theodora)* That's it! Offer to have sex with him!

Angela: Ew!

Veronica: *(Sitting up)* I think that's wrong, Mrs. Hunter! I'd stand up for Harry, if I could stand up.

Franklin: Very, maybe if you and Theodora work together...

Angela: Now it's a conspiracy? Way to feed dad's paranoia!

Franklin: Like your behavior does him any good!

Theodora: I think you're onto something, Franklin! I think the only hope for bringing Harry and AAC into the twenty-first century is for the three of us to work together!

Harry: I suppose you're going to take the company away from me, install Franklin as president, and then have a three-way on the desk!

Angela: Do you really think this is a wholesome enough environment to raise me in, Dad?

Patricia and Anthony enter, both a little looped. Patricia whirls about as if dancing, Anthony partnering her in an impromptu pas de deux as they sing "Shimmy, Shimmy, Ko-Ko-Bop."

Harry: Mom! Have you been drinking, too?

Patricia: Oh no, Harry! I've been drinking three! Oh, Anthony!

She giggles, kisses Anthony on the cheek. He blushes.

Anthony: Patricia, control yourself! People are watchin'!

Harry: Oh my god! Dad was right! You're sleeping with my mom!

Anthony: Watch your mouth, son! I got more respect for Patricia than that, and for your dead father!

Harry: But you've got no respect for me!

Anthony: Why would I have any respect for you?

Patricia: Anthony...

Anthony: All right. For your mother's sake, I have the utmost respect for you.

Patricia: But we will sleep together soon, won't we, Anthony? *(To the rest)* Over lunch, he proposed! We're engaged!

Veronica, Franklin, Theodora, and Angela: Congratulations!

Harry: Where's the ring?

Anthony: Who cares about a little t'ing like a ring?

Theodora: Well, at least now there'll be one man in the family who knows how to earn a living!

Harry: Mom! How can you do this to dad?

Patricia: He's dead, dear. You do remember that?

Harry: But you're marrying a mobster! He wants to take over AAC! He's out to destroy me!

Anthony: Why would I want to hurt you, son? You're a good guy—misguided, but good. And you know I loved your father. He was always aces with me!

Angela: I think you should let him help you, Dad. There's no one else to turn to.

Harry: You want me to pursue this path of criminality?

Anthony: I'm only too happy to show you the way!

The telephone rings. Everyone looks at it.

Veronica: *(Answering)* Good afternoon, Veronica Arcade Company, AAC speaking. How may you direct me?
(Presses phone to her chest)
It's Mr. Paster from Out-of-the-Brew!

Everyone watches anxiously as Harry takes the phone.

Harry: Mr. Paster, I mean Brewster! Harry Hunter here! Yes, nice finally to speak to you, too!
(Signals to others that he's got this under control)
Yes, I was pretty pleased with our proposal as well. I know

that AAC and Out-of-the-Past can do great things together!...
I know it's a big job, Mr. Brewster, but I'm confident we can
deliver. I mean, look at the numbers! With the kind of investment
we're talking about, AAC will be able to retool our
manufacturing lines and at least double, maybe triple, our
capacity!... Wait, what? No, that's just not true! I don't even
know where you'd get such an idea... Well, Mr. Brewster, you
can't believe everything you hear, and I assure you... I'm sorry,
that's just not gonna happen. This is a family operation, Mr.
Brewster, and he's part of the family! No! No! I don't care what
you say, I won't fire Repairman Dan! I'd rather see the whole
operation go up in flames! Oh yeah? Well fuck you, too!
(Harry slams down the phone as others gasp, looks sheepishly at them as they stare at him in disbelief)
I guess that's not gonna happen.
(Others sigh)
We'll just have to find another way!

Anthony: Wait just a goddamn minute! Are you tellin' me Repairman Dan's your only problem, all that stands between you and a multi-million-dollar opportunity?

Harry: Yes, he did express some concern about Repairman Dan...

Anthony: Son, say the word and that problem goes away!

Harry: I don't want that problem to go away, and neither would my dad!

Anthony: Son, I don't think you're dealin' with reality!

Harry: Well what if I don't want to deal with reality? What has reality ever done for me? Took away my father in his prime! Turned my mother into a grasping, lascivious whore!

Anthony: Hey!

Harry: Turned both my wife and daughter against me—my Angel, who's now stoned out of her gourd, with a ring through her nose! Even Veronica doesn't really understand what I'm trying to do here or she would never have tried to get me to hire Franklin at a moment like this. The only person I can trust is Repairman Dan!

Patricia: Well, things can't go on like this, honey. What do you intend to do?

Harry: I guess I've got to let the business go. It's obvious I can't run it. And I can't sell it. Who would buy it?

Anthony: I'll be happy to take it off your hands!

Harry: Thanks, Anthony, no. I still want some good to come of it!

Angela: That just doesn't seem possible, Dad.

Harry: I know, but maybe there's a way. Maybe if I give AAC to someone, or some people, who have nothing, historically speaking; do my little bit to try to make up for this country's original sin...

Franklin: You mean slavery?

Harry: No, Franklin. I mean something before that: genocide! I want to give AAC to the Native Americans. They're already into gaming, anyway, with their casinos. And I know the perfect person...

All but Harry: Who?

Harry: Repairman Dan!

Theodora: Repairman Dan is a Native American?

Anthony: Jeez, I didn't know he was an Indian! No wonder he can't hold his liquor: it's biological! But, I'm sorry son. Speakin' on behalf of my bride-to-be and me, we just can't let you get away with this!

A knock on the door. Dr. Frechette enters.

Harry: Dr. Frechette! What are you doing here?

Dr. Frechette: You mean you haven't told him?

Anthony: Not yet.

Harry: Told me what?

Anthony: Look, son, I'm sorry, but your mom and me made more than one decision over lunch...

The ATTENDANT enters, carrying a straitjacket. He bears a striking resemblance to Ray.

Harry: Daddy?

Attendant: Excuse me?

Dr. Frechette: He's in worse shape than I thought!

Harry: Wait! You're joking, right? I mean, you can't just have me put away! There are laws, aren't there?

Anthony: Oh yeah, there are laws, but if your shrink thinks it's right and your family agrees...

Harry: Are you kidding me? Mom, did you agree to this?
(Patricia looks away)
Theo, surely you won't let this happen?

Theodora: Sorry, Harry. I think it's for the best.

Harry: Angela, love?

Angela: Dad, I'm a minor. It's not up to me.

Harry: Veronica, won't even you stand up for me?

Veronica: I have no legal standing, Mr. Hunter. And I'm still having a little trouble standing.

Franklin: Also, it's not in her best interest.

Harry: All right! Fine! Whatever! I agree! Anthony, you can be my silent partner!

Anthony: It's too late for that, son. This is out of my hands!

Harry: But wasn't this all your idea?

Anthony: You'll have to ask your mother.

Harry: Mom?

Patricia: Oh, Harry. If only you had listened to me. Veronica, you'll stay on, won't you? I need someone with a working knowledge of the business, such as it is.

Veronica: Of course, Mrs. Hunter!

Harry: Veronica!

Patricia: And Franklin, I think you're the perfect person to make everything right for our customers. You're only a boy to me, but you're more of a man than my son will ever be!

Harry: Mom!

Franklin: Whatever you say, Mrs. Hunter!

Patricia: Theodora, I know we've had our differences, but now that I understand all you've been through, putting up with my son and still somehow raising such a beautiful girl... Just know, you'll be well taken care of!

Theodora: Sounds good to me!

Angela: What about me, grandma?

Patricia: Tell you what: you take that ring out of your nose and you'll be well taken care of, too!

Angela: Will do! Thanks, grandma. I love you! *(Hugs her)*

Patricia: You see the irony, don't you, Dr. Frechette? Harry's problem all along really was his mother!

Harry: No! This just can't be! You're all against me!

> *Harry runs to the wall, grabs the toy rifle, trains it on everyone. Anthony removes it from his hands.*

Anthony: It's a good thing this is only a toy, kid. Otherwise, not even Patricia could keep me from murderin' you!

Harry: It's an exact replica...

Dr. Frechette: *(To the Attendant)* Walter.
(The Attendant approaches Harry with the straitjacket. Harry begins to resist)
Franklin, could you help him?
(Franklin helps subdue Harry, who struggles ineffectually)
I'm afraid any judge will agree, Harry, you show the classic signs of paranoia.

Harry: So you're against me, too! You don't understand me at all!

Dr. Frechette: Please, Harry. I'm so far inside your head, I hear the voices you do!

Harry: But my enemies are real! You're one of them! So are you all! All of you have betrayed me!

Patricia: Nonsense, dear. I'm your mother. How could I betray you?

Harry is now straitjacketed.

Anthony: Get him outta here! I won't have him disturbin' my fiancé any further!

Harry: This is all your fault, Little Anthony! My mother would never have agreed to such a thing if it weren't for you!

Anthony: You really got a mouth on you, kid, just like your dad. That's what caused all the trouble. And no one wants to see you end up like him!

Dr. Frechette: He means dead, Harry. Not that we don't all die, anyway.

Harry: Thanks for letting me know! So that's it, isn't it, Anthony? Mystery solved. You killed my father! Admit it!

Anthony: Look, kid, I'd like to help you out here, I really would. I appreciate your psychological difficulties. But let's get real: there's no statute of limitations on murder. So you can assume I shot your father in the head if it makes you feel better, but I can't tell you that!

Harry: *(To Patricia)* And you're okay with this? You're going to marry your husband's killer?

Patricia: Oh, Harry, you have no idea how annoying your father could be!

The lights dim on all but Harry.

Harry:
I always knew that it would come to this.
There was no other way for this to end.
The world isn't really a happy place,
No matter our efforts to make it so.
We try to fill the world with joy and love;
But, like all the rest, they're only fleeting.
The only thing that counts is that we try,
Bow to reality with heads held high.
Pain and suffering, sickness, hate, and war,
Violence—physical, emotional—

Are our inheritance and legacy.
How can art and science stand against them?
I've done my best to pursue my beliefs.
Though my success is small, I feel no shame.
Shame remains with those who stood against me.
I'm only human. They must live with that.

The lights return as Patricia snaps her fingers. Dr. Frechette and the Attendant take Harry away.

Patricia: Veronica, get Mr. Brewster on the line.

Veronica: Right away, Mrs. Hunter!

As Veronica does...

Anthony: *(To Patricia)* You done the right thing, sweetheart.

Patricia: You don't have to tell me that!

Veronica: Mr. Brewster for you, Mrs. Hunter!

Patricia: *(Taking the phone)* Mr. Brewster? Pat Hunter here, from the American Arcade Company. Yes, I thought you should know my son Harry's decided to retire and AAC is in the best of hands: my own. That's right, Mr. Brewster. It's a brand new day and AAC's ready to do business. I understand the only real problem you have with our proposal is Repairman Dan? Well, I'm the kind of chief executive who makes problems like that go away.
(Snaps her fingers. Anthony pulls out a cellphone, quietly makes a call)
So, Mr. Brewster, ready to take a shot with AAC? Excellent! Let the games begin!

Blackout.

About the Author

Steven Samuels, a writer, director, actor, producer, editor, and publisher with a bad habit of co-founding theater companies, managed and occasionally acted with New York's renowned avant-garde comic troupe, The Ridiculous Theatrical Company; was senior editor of TCG Books and *American Theatre* magazine; and served as an artistic associate at Arena Stage in Washington, D.C. A graduate of Bennington College and Brown University, he has edited scores of publications, including *The Complete Plays of Charles Ludlam, Ridiculous Theatre: Scourge of Human Folly, Ridiculous!: The Theatrical Life and Times of Charles Ludlam,* and works by Jon Robin Baitz, Eric Bogosian, Constance Congdon, Richard Foreman, Tony Kushner, Suzan-Lori Parks, Reynolds Price, Ronald Ribman, José Rivera, Stephen Sondheim, Paula Vogel, and George C. Wolfe, among others. The recipient of writing fellowships from the New York State Council on the Arts and the Harry Frank Guggenheim Foundation, he has, in various capacities, been involved in more than 70 world premiere stage productions, including his own *When Jekyll Met Hyde, The Last Laugh, Love Among the Frankensteins, Evening the Score, The Man with the Birdcage on His Head, The Merchant of Asheville, The Improbables,* and *American Arcade.* A Brooklyn native, he lives in Asheville, NC, where he serves as the producing artistic director and publisher of The Sublime Theater & Press.

CPSIA information can be obtained
at www.ICGtesting.com
Printed in the USA
BVHW031015010621
608546BV00003B/682